# Under the Sea

# Dolphins

by Carol K. Lindeen

Consulting Editor: Gail Saunders-Smith, PhD

Consultant: Jody Rake, Member
Southwest Marine/Aquatic Educator's Association

Capstone
press

Mankato, Minnesota

Pebble Plus is published by Capstone Press,
151 Good Counsel Drive, P.O. Box 669, Mankato, Minnesota 56002.
www.capstonepress.com

1 2 3 4 5 6 09 08 07 06 05 04

*Library of Congress Cataloging-in-Publication Data*
Lindeen, Carol K., 1976–
   Dolphins / by Carol K. Lindeen.
   p. cm.—(Pebble Plus: Under the sea)
   Includes bibliographical references (p. 23) and index.
   ISBN-13: 978-0-7368-2599-3 (hardcover)     ISBN-10: 0-7368-2599-1 (hardcover)
   ISBN-13: 978-0-7368-5111-4 (softcover pbk.)     ISBN-10: 0-7368-5111-9 (softcover pbk.)
   1. Dolphins—Juvenile literature. [1. Dolphins.] I. Title. II. Series.
QL737.C432L545 2005
599.53—dc22                                        2003025609

Summary: Simple text and photographs present the lives of dolphins.

**Editorial Credits**
Martha E. H. Rustad, editor; Juliette Peters, designer; Kelly Garvin, photo researcher;
   Karen Hieb, product planning editor

**Photo Credits**
Corbis/SeaWorld of California, cover
Creatas, 1
Jeff Rotman, 18–19
Minden Pictures/Norbert Wu, 4–5, 16–17; Flip Nicklin, 12–13; Konrad Wothe, 20–21
Seapics.com/Doug Perrine, 8–9; Tim Calver, 10–11; Masa Ushioda, 14–15
Tom Stack & Associates/Brian Parker, 6–7

## Note to Parents and Teachers

The Under the Sea series supports national science standards related to the diversity
and unity of life. This book describes and illustrates dolphins. The images support
early readers in understanding the text. The repetition of words and phrases helps early
readers learn new words. This book also introduces early readers to subject-specific
vocabulary words, which are defined in the Glossary section. Early readers may need
assistance to read some words and to use the Table of Contents, Glossary, Read More,
Internet Sites, and Index/Word List sections of the book.

**Word Count: 91**
**Early-Intervention Level: 13**

# Table of Contents

# Dolphins

What are dolphins?

Dolphins are mammals.

Dolphins breathe air.

They have blowholes

on top of their heads.

Small dolphins are about as long as a bicycle. Big dolphins are about as long as a school bus.

# Swimming

Dolphins swim fast
through the water.
Dolphins move their tails
up and down to swim.

Dolphins steer with their flippers.

Dolphins jump out
of the water. Dolphins
play together.

# Hunting

Dolphins dive
to hunt for food.

Dolphins catch fish and other animals with their teeth. Dolphins swallow their food whole.

# Under the Sea

Dolphins swim together
under the sea.

# Glossary

blowhole—a hole on top of a dolphin's head; dolphins breathe air through blowholes.

dive—to go down into water headfirst

flipper—a flat limb with bones on the bodies of some sea animals; dolphins have two flippers; flippers help dolphins swim.

hunt—to find and kill animals for food

mammal—a warm-blooded animal with a backbone that breathes air with lungs; mammals have some hair or fur; female mammals feed milk to their young.

steer—to move in a certain direction

# Read More

**Greenberg, Daniel A.** *Dolphins.* Animalways. New York: Benchmark Books, 2003.

**Hirschmann, Kris.** *Dolphins.* Creatures of the Sea. San Diego: Kidhaven Press, 2004.

**Spilsbury, Louise, and Richard Spilsbury.** *A School of Dolphins.* Animal Groups. Chicago: Heinemann Library, 2004.

# Internet Sites

FactHound offers a safe, fun way to find Internet sites related to this book. All of the sites on FactHound have been researched by our staff.

Here's how:

1. Visit *www.facthound.com*

2. Type in this special code **0736825991** for age-appropriate sites. Or enter a search word related to this book for a more general search.

3. Click on the **Fetch It** button.

FactHound will fetch the best sites for you!

# Index/Word List